The
George Lozuks:
Doers of the Word

ROBERTA RYAN
Illustrated by John Ham

To
George and Veda Rae Lozuk,
faithful doers of God's Word,
their children,
Paul, Mark, Ann, Larry, and Lolly,
and granddaughter,
Kimberly Ann

© Copyright 1985 • Broadman Press
All rights reserved
4242-93
ISBN: 0-8054-4293-6

Dewey Decimal Classification: J266.092
Subject Headings: LOZUK, GEORGE / / LOZUK, VEDA / / MISSIONS—
VENEZUELA / / MISSIONS—ECUADOR
Library of Congress Catalog Card Number: 85-6615
Printed in the United States of America

Library of Congress Cataloging in Publication Data
Ryan, Roberta, 1921-
  The George Lozuks.

  1. Lozuk, George—Juvenile literature. 2. Lozuk,
Veda Rae—Juvenile literature. 3. Missionaries—Ecuador
—Biography—Juvenile literature. 4. Missionaries—
Venezuela—Biography—Juvenile literature.
5. Missionaries—United States—Biography—Juvenile
literature. 6. Missions—Ecuador—Juvenile literature.
7. Missions—Venezuela—Juvenile literature. I. Ham,
John. II. Title.
BV2853.E3L697 1985   266'.0092'2 [B]   85-6615
ISBN 0-8054-4293-6

Contents

Right-Hand Tagalong

George slipped an arm around Papa Lozuk's waist. In his other hand George carried Papa Lozuk's briefcase. Papa Lozuk hugged George's shoulder, and together they strode down the wide sidewalk.

Papa Lozuk was pastor of the Russian Baptist Church in Fort Worth, Texas. Everywhere he went, it seemed George was by his side. "A regular right-hand tagalong," his family said. But George did not mind. He liked doing things with his father.

"Papa," George said one day, "how big were you when you came to America?"

"Just a bit bigger than you," his father said. "Times were hard in White Russia. I came to America to earn money and help my family."

"Were you a preacher then?" George asked.

"No. I was not even a Christian when I came to America," Papa Lozuk said. "But I hadn't been here long when a lady sat by me on the streetcar. She invited me to the Slavic Baptist mission. She said some of the people spoke Russian, so I accepted her invitation. I liked what the pastor said about God's love. Soon after that I became a Christian and was baptized."

"Was that mission the same as our church now?" George asked.

"Yes. Only then it was much smaller. But we told people about Jesus. God helped us. The mission grew and grew. Before long it was big enough to be a church."

"I like our church," George said. "I like to hear you preach in Russian. I like to hear the people sing in Russian and in Polish."

"And sometimes in Czech and Greek and English," Papa Lozuk added.

"And all at the same time!" George laughed.

As usual, it was still early when George and his parents got to church on Sunday morning. While his father checked to see that everything was ready for Sunday School, George dusted the pews. He dusted the piano and pulpit, too.

Soon the people began to arrive. They hugged each other like members of one big, happy family.

Mama Lozuk's sister was George's Sunday School teacher. The summer he was ten years old, she talked to the children about trusting Jesus.

"You children have heard us tell about Jesus. You know that he wants you to love him. He will forgive you of all the wrong things you have done. But you must ask him to. He wants you to decide for yourself that you will trust him and live for him."

George thought about what his aunt said. Even during the worship service, he thought about it. Then, as the people around him sang the last hymn, George asked God to forgive him of everything he had done wrong. He told Jesus that he would live for him.

He knew then that he was ready to join the church. Some of his friends in Sunday School made the same decision. They all went to the front of the church at the end of the worship service to show that they had already trusted

Jesus. They told the pastor that they wanted to be members of the church.

At the next business meeting, the church members asked George and his friends many questions.

"Why do you want to be baptized?" someone asked.

"I am trusting in Jesus," George answered. "I want to be baptized like he was."

"Has Jesus forgiven your sins?" another asked.

"Yes, sir," George replied.

"What are your plans now?" still another asked.

"I want to live like Jesus," George said.

The church voted to let George and his friends be baptized. A few days later, George's father baptized them. Now, they were members of the Russian Baptist Church of Fort Worth.

One Sunday, after church, one of the ladies hugged George. George cringed. "I hope she doesn't rumple my hair today," he thought to himself. But she did.

"You're going to be a preacher just like your father when you grow up, aren't you?" she said.

"No, Ma'am," he wanted to say. "A scientist, maybe, but not a preacher. I'm proud my father is a preacher, but that is not for me." But he couldn't say that to the lady. He just smoothed his hair and smiled.

George was always doing something at church. Now, people were asking him to do even more. One day the pianist said, "You play the violin, don't you?"

"Yes, Ma'am," George answered. "I learned to play it at school."

"Would you like to play in our church orchestra?" the lady said.

"I surely would," George replied. He knew it wasn't really an orchestra. The orchestra included the lady who played the piano and two men who played handsaws. The

saws were played with violin bows. The music sounded sort of like a pipe organ. George's violin became the fourth instrument. Their music helped the people worship God.

George also sang in the choir.

"I remember the first time you sang at church," Mama Lozuk said. "You were two years old. You stood in front of all the people and sang 'Jesus Loves Me.' God gave you a good voice. You must always use it to help others."

"God has given you a good mind, too," Papa Lozuk said. "You must study and make good grades. If you work hard, you can make all A's. You have good teachers. They can help you learn many things."

"Yes, Sir," George said. "I will."

The summer before George finished high school, he worked at night for the city newspaper. During the day he went to summer school.

At summer school George met Jesse Strong. Jesse was a member of another church.

One day Jesse said, "George, classes will be over soon. Why don't you go with me to our church camp?"

George wasn't sure what camp would be like, but he liked the idea.

"Papa," George said that night, "Jesse wants me to go to church camp with him. Will that be all right?"

"I see no problem," Papa Lozuk said. So, George went to camp.

Jesse and George spread their quilts under a big tree. At night, they looked up at the stars and talked about God.

"George," Jesse said, "I think God is calling me to be a preacher. Will you help me pray that he will show me what he wants me to do?"

Every day George and Jesse prayed. Every day they listened to the camp pastor talk about obeying God.

The last day Jesse said, "Thank you, George, for praying with me. I think now that God does not want me to preach."

"Maybe he wants you to do something else," George said. But George was very quiet. He was beginning to feel that God wanted him to preach.

The camp pastor preached the last sermon. Then he invited the young people to make decisions for God. George left his seat beside Jesse. He walked to the front and spoke to the pastor.

"I think God wants me to do something special," he said. "I'm not sure what it is. But whatever it is, I want to do it."

George finished high school in January 1945. He was sixteen years old, and his grades were the third highest in his class.

A large oil company heard about George's good record as a student.

"We want you to work for us," the manager said. "We will train you for the job and pay you a good salary."

"Thank you," George said. "Please, let me think about it."

That night, George couldn't sleep. "What should I do?" he kept asking himself. "The oil company will train me, if I work for them. But if I am going to be a preacher, I need to go to college. I need to learn how to be a good preacher."

All night George tossed and turned in his bed. He also prayed. He remembered what his mother had told him. "When you were born, all the family knelt around your bed," she had said. "Your father thanked God for you. He asked God to let us help you grow in wisdom, and in knowledge, and in favor with God and man. Then, when you were one month old, we took you to church. It was Christmas. Again, we thanked God for you. You were the best gift we ever had."

George thought about a little plaque on his wall. His father had brought it home from a meeting in a faraway city. Even in the dark, George knew what it said.

Only one life, 'twill soon be past;
Only what's done for Christ will last.

At last George fell asleep. The next day, he went to see the manager of the oil company.

"Thank you for the job you offered me," he said. "But I cannot accept it. God has called me to preach. I must go to college and learn to be a preacher."

"We will miss you," the manager said. "But you will make a good preacher. Thank you for telling me."

"I still don't know what college God wants me to go to," George confided to a preacher friend.

"I am going to visit Baylor University in Waco, Texas, next Saturday," the friend said. "Why don't you go with me? Baylor is a Baptist school, you know."

The trip to Waco was the longest ride George could remember. Almost ninety miles in one day!

As George and his friend walked around the campus, they met one of the students.

"I think you should come to Baylor," the student said. "We need young men like you."

That was it! George was Baylor-bound.

Mama Lozuk helped George pack a footlocker and a big suitcase. Mama and Papa Lozuk drove George to Baylor.

"We'll miss you," Mama Lozuk said, as they left.

"We will pray for you," Papa Lozuk promised. "And I will write a letter to you every day."

"Thank you, Papa. I'll miss both of you," George said as he hugged them good-bye. "Thank you for all you have done for me."

11

Chuckles

"Hurry, Daddy! It's my birthday and time to get the Christmas tree," Veda Rae called.

"Just a minute, Chuckles. I'll be right there," Mr. Tyson answered.

Veda Rae chuckled. Every year on her birthday, December 14, her father took her and her sisters to buy a Christmas tree.

"Hurry, Mickey! Hurry, Elouise!" she called to her sisters. "It's time to get the Christmas tree."

Soon the girls were riding down the street with their father. At the Christmas tree lot, Veda Rae saw many trees. Some were small, but many were taller than her father. It was hard to choose the right one. At last she saw it, fluffy and round and thick. Daddy paid the man and tied the tree to the top of the car.

At home, the girls helped set the tree in the living room. Around and around they went, talking, chuckling, and hanging decorations on the tree.

"I wonder if I'll get a Shirley Temple doll for Christmas," Elouise said.

"Me, too," Mickey said. Mickey could not talk plainly nor learn as quickly as her sisters, but she knew what she wanted for Christmas.

"I want a Shirley Temple doll, too," Veda Rae said.

On Christmas morning three Shirley Temple dolls sat under the Christmas tree. And three happy girls danced around the room.

Weeks turned into months, and then it was summer. The Tyson family was off to the sandy beach. While the girls built castles in the sand, the rest of the family waded and fished in the warm water.

"I want to help you clean the fish," Veda Rae said to her mother. And she did. Mother dropped them into the skillet to fry. Daddy nibbled one of the fish. Then he took a big bite. "This has to be the best eating to be found anywhere," he said.

Driving home late at night, Daddy sang to Veda Rae while the others slept. Sometimes Veda Rae sang with him. He had a strong voice and sang in the choir at Morgan Avenue Baptist Church in Corpus Christi.

The summer Veda Rae was eight years old, she went to a revival meeting at her church. She listened to all the preacher said.

"I think the preacher is talking to me," she said to herself. "I need to ask Jesus to forgive me."

But when the preacher gave the invitation, Veda Rae held to the pew in front of her. She wanted to turn loose and publicly accept Jesus as her Savior. But she didn't. Every night of the revival she felt the same way until on the last night, she accepted Jesus as her Savior.

"I wonder if people like Mickey can be saved," Veda Rae thought.

When she got home, she talked to Mickey. "Jesus loves you, Mickey. Do you love Jesus?" she said.

"No," Mickey said. But Veda Rae knew she was teasing. She didn't know what she was saying. But it bothered Veda Rae, anyway.

14

Every day Veda Rae prayed for Mickey. She asked God to help Mickey be like other children. Then one day, as Veda Rae prayed, God seemed to say, "I will take care of Mickey."

Later Veda Rae talked to her mother. "God does not always answer my prayers exactly like I want him to, does he?" she said.

"But God always knows what is best," her mother replied.

In high school Veda Rae helped edit the school newspaper. What fun it was to write the stories instead of just reading them! That year she also went to a meeting of the Texas Interscholastic League. When she got home, she announced, "Now, I know what I want to do when I finish high school. I want to study journalism at the University of Texas."

Veda Rae sent a letter to the university. But when the answer came, it said, "We regret there is no more room."

"No room," Veda Rae moaned. "They don't have room for me."

For once, Veda Rae did not chuckle.

"Why don't you enroll in Del Mar Junior College here in Corpus Christi," her mother suggested.

"But I want to go to the University of Texas," Veda Rae insisted. "Del Mar is too close to home."

"I know," Mother said, "but Del Mar would be a start."

"I'll think about it," Veda Rae said. But she felt grumpy.

A few days later, she asked her mother to go with her to enroll at Del Mar.

While Veda Rae studied at Del Mar, she worked with the youth group at church. She also sang in the choir. Many times she met with church leaders to study the Bible and pray.

"Search for God's will in your life," the leaders said. "If

you ask him, he will show you what he wants you to do."

"Do you suppose he would hear me if I ask him where I should go to college next year?" Veda Rae asked.

"Yes," the youth leader said. "God can let you know where he wants you to study."

Veda Rae prayed and waited. Then, one day, she learned some facts about Baylor University in Waco, Texas.

"Baylor is a Baptist school," she said. "I can study journalism there. Maybe God wants me to go to Baylor."

Veda Rae sat down and wrote a letter to Baylor. This time she was accepted. "I think this is what God wanted me to do all along," she chuckled.

The weeks passed quickly. As she waved good-bye to her family, she knew she would miss them. But again she chuckled. She was off to Baylor University. God had led her all the way.

Baylor Days

While George studied at Baylor University, he preached almost every Sunday. Also, on Friday nights, he led a tiny mission near the campus. His friends worked in other missions nearby. Once a month they met together to pray and sing and tell Bible stories.

One evening when they were all together, George noticed a young lady who was helping. He saw the friendly help she gave each child. "Why can't I meet a girl like her?" he thought. "I want to know her."

Later, George asked his friend, "Who is the young lady who helps you at your mission?"

"That's Veda Rae Tyson," his friend said. "She is a sophomore, but she's new here. She went to Del Mar last year."

The more George thought about it, the more he wanted to meet Veda Rae. One Saturday he went to the dormitory where she lived.

"I'm George Lozuk," he said. "I hear you are a sophomore."

"Yes, I am," Veda Rae said.

"Will you help us build our sophomore float for the homecoming parade?" George asked.

"I'll be glad to," Veda Rae said. She wasn't sure what it was all about, but she knew she wanted to know this handsome young man.

It was not long before George invited Veda Rae to go with him to the sophomore banquet. After that they dated each other often.

George moved into the home of Dr. and Mrs. Wilson Fielder. The Fielders had been missionaries in China for many years. They helped George to see that there are people all around the world who need to know Jesus.

Later, there was a revival meeting at Emmanual Baptist Church, near the Baylor campus. The visiting preacher was W. W. Enete. George went to every service. Dr. Enete was a missionary to Brazil. He told about many people who had never heard about Jesus.

During the last night of the revival meetings, Dr. Enete gave an invitation. George walked down the aisle and shook his hand. "I am already a Christian, Dr. Enete. Now, I think God wants me to be a missionary," he said. "I'm not sure where he wants me to go. Wherever it is, I'm ready."

Soon, it was vacation time. George went to California to work for the Home Mission Board. He helped in camps, led Vacation Bible Schools, and preached in revivals. He talked to many people about Jesus.

Veda Rae returned to her home in Corpus Christi. All summer she worked as a secretary in her church. One letter she typed bothered her. It announced an upcoming revival meeting.

"I want us to have the revival," she said. "But I don't want to go. If I do, I know I must tell the people that God wants me to be a missionary. I'm not sure I'm ready to do that."

But the day for the revival came. The last night, Veda Rae walked down the aisle.

"God wants me to be a missionary," she told her pastor. "I am ready to go wherever he wants me to go."

She looked around. Twenty of her friends were following her. Some of them were members of her Sunday School class. They, too, wanted to obey God. Veda Rae was glad she had decided to tell the church that God wanted her to be a missionary.

At home, Veda Rae's mother said, "I don't want you to go to some far-off country to be a missionary."

Veda Rae was sad. She wanted to please her mother, but she knew she must obey God.

A few days later, her mother said, "I'm sorry I said that about your being a missionary. If that is what God wants you to do, I promise to do everything I can to help you be the best missionary you can be."

"Thank you," Veda Rae said. She gave her mother a big hug. "And thank you, God," she prayed. "Thank you for helping my mother understand."

Summer was almost over. Veda Rae wanted to go back to Baylor. But her father and her younger sister were ill. Doctor bills were expensive.

"Maybe I should stay at home and work this year," she said.

"No," her mother said. "You must go back. When you were born, I bought an insurance policy for you. We will cash it. You can use the money to go back to Baylor."

Veda Rae returned to Baylor. Just as she finished using the insurance money, the editor of the Baylor annual called. "We want you to be our assistant editor," he said. "We will pay you $40 a month."

When George returned to Baylor, a small church in Manor, Texas, asked him to be their pastor.

"If I am going to be a pastor," George said, "I need to be ordained."

Papa and Mama Lozuk traveled from Fort Worth for the

ordination service. Papa preached the special sermon. Then George knelt by the pulpit. All the preachers passed by and put their hands on his head. This showed that they wished him well in his new work for the Lord. Each one said a special prayer for George. "Thank you, God," George prayed. "Please help me be a good pastor."

All too soon it was graduation day. Veda Rae and George received their diplomas. Then Veda Rae returned to Corpus Christi. She planned to teach journalism in a small college there. But George stayed at Baylor. He wanted to take some extra classes. Also, he was still pastor of the Manor Baptist Church.

It was hard to say good-bye. But George and Veda Rae promised to keep in touch.

California Honeymoon

"Veda Rae," George wrote, "I want you to go with me to Fort Worth. I want you to meet my family."

Veda Rae sang as she packed her suitcase. She had met Papa and Mama Lozuk when they went to Baylor for George's ordination. But she had not visited in their home.

Veda Rae met George at Baylor and together they drove to Fort Worth. Papa and Mama Lozuk met them with hugs and a big welcome. Veda Rae met the rest of George's family. On Sunday, she went with them to the little Russian church. She was glad she could hear Papa Lozuk preach. "What a wonderful family!" she said. "I like them, every one."

In the afternoon, as George and Veda Rae drove through a big park, they stopped under a tree.

"Veda Rae," George said. "I've been thinking. I want to go back to California this summer. But . . ."

George was quiet a moment. Veda Rae waited. "I'll miss you," she started to say. "California is such a long way from Texas."

"But I don't want to go alone," George said. "I want you to go with me."

"You mean you want us to get married so we can go together?" Veda Rae asked.

George nodded.

"Oh, George. That's wonderful! We can marry and the trip to California can be our honeymoon."

The weekend passed quickly. George returned to his studies at Baylor. Veda Rae went back to teaching in Corpus Christi.

George tried to study, but he kept thinking about Veda Rae. One evening he walked to town. He looked at the diamond rings in a store window. They sparkled like the stars in the sky. Inside, George picked a ring he was sure Veda Rae would like. He paid the clerk and she wrapped the ring in a tiny box. George tucked it in his pocket.

Back in his room, George studied until midnight. But he couldn't keep his mind on what he was reading. He put his books away, got in his car, and started toward Corpus Christi. A heavy fog slowed him down, but he felt the ring in his pocket and sang a happy song. He reached Corpus Christi just as the sun was coming up.

Later, George and Veda Rae strolled along the beach. George took the ring out of his pocket and showed it to Veda Rae.

"Oh, George! It's beautiful!" she said.

George slipped the ring on Veda Rae's finger.

They set the wedding for Friday, June 2, 1950, at the Morgan Avenue Baptist Church in Corpus Christi. George's father performed the ceremony. And as Veda Rae walked down the aisle with her father, George sang to her, "I Love You Truly."

Outside, their friends showered them with rice. They had already decorated George's car with paint, ribbons, and empty cans. But George and Veda Rae escaped in her father's car.

From Corpus Christi, the newlyweds drove to their little church in Manor, Texas. George preached on Sunday, and on Monday they drove on to Fort Worth. After a brief visit

with Papa and Mama Lozuk, they headed west to California and their first missionary assignment. During the engagement period, Veda Rae had gotten approved for the California assignment. By Monday morning they were ready to start to work.

"This is Mr. and Mrs. Lozuk," the pastor told the boys and girls in the Chinatown mission. "They are going to teach a Vacation Bible School for you."

"Lozuk! Lozuk!" the children repeated. "That's a funny name. Nah! We don't want it."

"What's your name?" Veda Rae asked a little girl.

"Pamela Wong," the girl said.

Veda Rae chuckled. "I like that name," she said. "And what's your name?" she asked a boy.

"Jimmy Su," the boy said.

"Hmmm. I like that name, too," Veda Rae said. "And I like you." She chuckled again.

Soon George and Veda Rae and all the boys and girls were laughing. By the time Vacation Bible School was over they were good friends.

"We don't want you to go," the children begged. "We like you. We like to sing the songs with you. We like to hear the Bible stories. We want you to stay."

But George and Veda Rae had other Vacation Bible Schools to teach in other California towns. All too soon, summer and the California honeymoon were over. It was time to go back to Texas—and school—again.

Ready! Get Set! Go!

"Come, live with us," Papa and Mama Lozuk said when George and Veda Rae returned to Fort Worth from California.

George and Veda Rae moved into the room that George had used when he was a boy. They enrolled at Southwestern Baptist Theological Seminary and drove across town to their classes.

Every Saturday they drove almost 200 miles to Manor, Texas. George was still pastor of the Manor Baptist Church. Veda Rae helped him visit the people. She taught a Sunday School class and played the piano. More and more people came to church. Many of them trusted Jesus as their Savior. The church grew and grew.

Every week the church paid George $30 for being their pastor. George and Veda Rae used their money carefully. First of all they took the tithe, a tenth, and gave it to the church.

"I still remember when I learned to tithe," Veda Rae said. "I was in high school and worked in a bakery. When Daddy saw my first check, he said, 'That's good. But now you have to pay a tithe to the church.' Then he thought a minute. 'No,' he said, 'I shouldn't say that, but the Bible teaches that you should, you know.' I knew that was true, and I've been tithing ever since."

But the money that Manor Baptist Church paid George each week was not enough. It had to pay for groceries, books, and many other things. And it had to pay for a tank of gas each week for the trip to Manor.

One week George did not have enough money to buy all the gas he needed. He bought what he could pay for, but the tank was not full.

"We'll go as far as we can," he said. "Maybe we can get to Manor. Then we can buy some more. We can pay for it when the church pays us."

George and Veda Rae started down the shortest road to Manor. They did not stop along the way. Just as they drove into Manor, they saw a service station.

"Let's stop for gas," George said. "I'm sure the tank must be empty."

"Will you let us have some gas if we promise to pay you after the church pays us?" George asked.

"Sure, Preacher. I'll trust you," answered the man who ran the station.

George watched the pump. Ten gallons, eleven, twelve, thirteen, four . . . te . . . en. The tank should hold only fourteen gallons, but the gas kept flowing. At last, at fourteen gallons and one pint, the pump stopped.

"God has really taken care of us. That tank was very empty! From now on, I must remember to save enough money to buy all the gas we need before leaving Fort Worth," George said.

For several months, George and Veda Rae lived with Papa and Mama Lozuk. They studied at the seminary and worked in the church at Manor.

"This is too much," Veda Rae said. "Why don't we move to Manor? We can rest from our studies. Next year we can come back to school."

"That's a good idea," George said.

George and Veda Rae moved to Manor, but by the next fall they had returned to the seminary. Again, every weekend they drove to Manor. In 1953 George graduated from the seminary. Once more they moved to Manor. George asked the church to help them find a house.

"I have two chicken houses," one of the members said. "We can clean them real good and put them together. We can put in a floor and install kitchen and bathroom fixtures. You will have a nice little house."

"That will be fine," George said. "The front room will be a bedroom and living room. The other one will be the kitchen and bath."

Veda Rae made curtains for their new house. She dyed them a bright blue. She hung pictures on the walls. The chicken-house house began to look like home. A year later their first son was born. They named him Paul. George and Veda Rae kept remembering that God had called them to be missionaries.

"But you can't be missionaries," the people said. "Where would Paul go to school? If he gets sick, what would you do?"

Sometimes George and Veda Rae wondered about it, too.

One day George said, "There's going to be a missions conference in Fort Worth. Why don't we go? Maybe God will help us know what he wants us to do."

George and Veda Rae bundled up Paul and drove to Fort Worth. After dinner with Papa and Mama Lozuk, they sat around the table eating cookies. Suddenly Paul coughed. His face turned red; then blue.

"He's choking!" everyone said at once.

"He swallowed a cookie crumb," Mama Lozuk said. "We must get it out."

George patted Paul on the back. Hard. Really hard. But

the crumb did not come out. He put his finger in Paul's mouth and tickled his throat.

"Oh, God, please make that crumb come out," Veda Rae prayed.

At last the crumb loosened. Paul's face turned white again. Then a rosy pink!

"Thank you, God, for saving Paul's life," the family prayed.

George and Veda Rae left Paul with Papa and Mama Lozuk. On their way to the missionary meeting, they passed a hospital.

Veda Rae looked at George. "You know," she said, "here we are four blocks from a big hospital and Paul almost died."

"There wasn't time to call a doctor. Not even an ambulance," George said. "Do you know what I'm thinking?"

"I think so," Veda Rae said. "God took care of Paul. If he can do that in Fort Worth, he can do it anywhere in the world."

"Maybe we should talk to the people from the Foreign Mission Board this afternoon," George said. "We can tell them God wants us to be missionaries."

"And that we know he will take care of us wherever we are," Veda Rae added.

After the missions conference, George, Veda Rae, and Paul returned to Manor. They waited and prayed. One day as Veda Rae was reading her Bible she discovered Deuteronomy 31:8. "The Lord, he it is that doth go before thee; he will be with thee, he will not fail thee, neither forsake thee: fear not, neither be dismayed." "If God wants us to be missionaries, he will prepare the way," she said to herself,

In February 1956 baby Mark was born. Then in May the

Foreign Mission Board appointed George and Veda Rae to be missionaries in Venezuela, South America.

"First of all, you must study Spanish so you can talk to the people in Venezuela. We will send you to language school in Costa Rica," the man at the Foreign Mission Board said. "You can study Spanish there."

In Costa Rica, George and Veda Rae found a new Baptist church in the city of San José (SAHN hoh-SAY).

"Even if I can't yet speak Spanish," Veda Rae said, "I can play the little pump organ."

"And we can make new friends," George said.

Weeks became months. George and Veda Rae learned to read and write and talk in Spanish.

Just before the end of school, George received a special message. "Your father is very ill," it said.

George talked to the director of the school. "Can you let us go home to Fort Worth early? My father is very sick."

"Yes," the director said. "The term is almost over, anyway."

George, Veda Rae, and the boys flew to Fort Worth. Papa Lozuk lived only a few more days.

Then with Spanish classes over it was time to go to Venezuela. With hugs and kisses and promises to write often, George and Veda Rae, Paul and Mark waved good-bye to their family and friends. They were off to Venezuela!

Hello, Venezuela

October 17, 1957!

After six days on the boat from New York, the Lozuks arrived in Caracas (Cah-RAH-cahs), Venezuela. George and Veda Rae looked around. Everything was new. Poinsettias were as big as trees. Climbing vines were heavy with purple flowers. Big houses, little houses were crowded close together on steep hillsides. And noise, noise was everywhere. Paul and Mark clapped their hands.

Some missionaries were waiting to meet them.

"Welcome to Venezuela," the missionaries said. "We want you to live in San Cristobal (SAHN crees-TOH-bahl). There are many small towns nearby that don't have a Baptist church at all. Maybe you can help start some missions."

"Sounds good," George said. "When do we start?"

"As soon as you are ready," one of the missionaries said. "I will go with you. I will help you find a house. Perhaps I can also help you get your driver's license."

For two days the missionaries bounced across rough country roads. Higher and higher into the mountains they went.

At last they reached San Cristobal. The Lozuks moved into a large house. Veda Rae hurried to unpack their suitcases. George made tables and cabinets with wood from their packing crates. And Paul and Mark explored the large yard. A few months later, Ann was born.

George soon discovered the missionaries and the churches in Venezuela were having problems. It was hard for the people to work together.

"We must be friends," George said. "We must ask God what to do." He opened his Bible to Psalm 37:5. "Commit thy way unto the Lord; trust also in him; and he shall bring it to pass," he read.

"That's true," Veda Rae said. "I remember how God helped us in Baylor and in Manor, Texas. I'm sure he will help us here."

Two months later George helped a pastor lead a revival in a nearby city. They preached every day in the city. Then they walked many miles into the country. They visited people in small villages. They slept in hammocks and fought the mosquitoes that buzzed around their heads. When they preached, many people listened. Some of them accepted Jesus as their Savior.

For a year and a half George and Veda Rae visited their neighbors. In December they helped prepare a Christmas program. George led the music, and Veda Rae played the piano. Soon many people were attending the church services.

"God is helping us," Veda Rae said. "I'm glad he brought us here."

Then it was time to move again. George, Veda Rae, and the children settled in Maracaibo (Mah-rah-CAH-ee-boh). It was a busy city near a large lake. Paul, Mark, and Ann liked to watch the ferry boats cross the lake each day. "Maybe we can ride the ferry someday," they said.

One day some people from Los Altos de Jalisco (LOHS AHL-tohs deh Jah-LEES-coh) Baptist Church visited George. "Will you be our pastor?" they said. "We have only

twenty members. But almost ninety people come to Sunday School."

"I would like to be your pastor," George said.

The church met in a tiny shack in a very poor part of the city. But when they had a revival, so many people attended the services they had to meet in the backyard. Almost twenty people trusted in Jesus.

One night George preached a sermon called "Can You Outgive God?" A young man listened carefully. When George gave the invitation, the young man accepted Jesus. "God has given me so much," he said, "I can't begin to repay him." The next day he took a friend to the revival meeting. "I want him to know Jesus, too," he said.

Soon it was Easter. The church had another revival, and a hundred people became Christians. The Los Altos de Jalisco church and other churches grew and grew.

One day George said, "I need to visit a pastor who lives on the other side of the lake. Would you like to ride the ferry boat with me?"

"Yes! Yes!" the boys exclaimed.

"Me, too," Ann said.

"I'll pack a lunch. We can have a picnic on the ferry boat," Veda Rae said.

While George and Veda Rae talked with the passengers on the ferry, the children played on deck. Later, at the church they made friends with the children in the yard while George talked to the pastor.

Not long afterward, George said to Veda Rae, "Have you noticed? The churches and missionaries are working together again. God is hearing our prayers."

"That's good," Veda Rae said. "God needs all of us to tell the people in Venezuela about Jesus."

Soon it was time for their furlough, a year back in the United States.

The Lozuks spent the year in Texas, visiting their family and friends. They told everyone about what God was doing in Venezuela. Then they returned to Venezuela. In 1964 baby Larry was born.

That same year all the churches in Venezuela had special revival meetings. They announced the services on the radio and TV and in the newspapers. Many people listened to the preachers. In one city, in just one service, five hundred persons accepted Jesus as their Savior. In other places, hundreds of people became Christians. Paul, Mark, and Ann also trusted Jesus as their Savior.

George and Veda Rae were happy. "God is doing great things for us, and we are glad," they said.

"Do you know what I want for my birthday?" Ann said. "I want a pet hamster!"

"All right," Veda Rae said. "But you must care for it."

"I will! I will!" Ann promised.

A week later the hamster disappeared. For two days everyone searched for it. Then, as suddenly as it had disappeared, the hamster sneaked out from under a kitchen cabinet.

Veda Rae picked it up, but the hamster bit her finger.

"Ouch!" she cried.

"You must see the doctor," her friends said. "The hamster may be sick."

When Veda Rae went to see the doctor, he said, "Yes, you must take the antirabies shots."

Before Veda Rae finished taking the shots, baby Martha was born. She was such a tiny baby. Her lungs were very small. Baby Martha lived only four days. Everyone was sad. Big tears rolled down George's cheeks as he carried the little white coffin to the cemetery.

"We do not understand why we had to lose her," Veda

Rae wrote to her friends. "But God knows. He has helped us in our sadness."

Sometime later, the missionaries asked George to go to a special meeting. When he returned, he said, "I'm sure we could tell many more people about Jesus if we had a good radio program."

"Will you start one for us?" the missionaries asked.

"Yes," George said. "I think that is what God wants me to do. While I am on furlough next year, I will learn how to do it. When we come back to Venezuela, I will help prepare programs for the radio. I am sure God will help us do it."

Egg-Carton Walls

After their next furlough in the United States, the Lozuks again returned to Venezuela.

Even before Veda Rae finished unpacking the furlough suitcases, George set his radio tape-recorder on a box in a small office near the back of the house. He hung bedspreads, curtains, and rugs on the walls. He even glued egg cartons on the walls. "They will soften the sounds," he said. "Maybe they will 'make-do' until we can get a real radio studio."

By Wednesday night, George and his radio recorder were ready. After prayer meeting at the church, a group of young people went home with him. They pushed the piano from the living room to the make-do studio. George adjusted the microphones.

"Ready!" he called. "It's time to record."

Four young women lined up behind one of the microphones. Four young men stood behind the other. The leader sat down at the piano. George waited for silence. Then he signaled. The music began. One of the young men preached. Another led the prayer. Still another made the announcements. The young women sang. George watched the controls. Only once or twice did he have to ask the group to correct a mistake.

Three hours later George looked at his watch. It was now

1:00 AM! "Good night, everybody!" he said. "Get a good night's sleep."

The next day George mailed the tape to a radio station on Bonaire (Bohn-AH-ee-reh) Island. The director listened to the tape. "I like that," he said. "It is by Venezuelans for Venezuelans. I think the people will like it."

Every week George taped a new radio program for the Baptist hour. It was called "Christ, the Only Hope." At the end of each program, he offered a Bible, a book, or a Bible study course to all who would write a letter to the radio station.

People all over the country listened to the programs. Some of them wrote letters to George.

One man wrote, "I heard your program on the radio. I accepted Jesus as my Savior. Thank you for your program. Can you, please, send me a Bible?"

Another letter arrived from some men in a jail. "A group of us listen to your program every week. Five of us have accepted Christ. Can you send us some books? We want to learn more about Jesus."

Still another man wrote from his home in the jungle. "Can you help me? I used to believe in many spirits. I used frogs and snakes to help me worship the spirits. But they did not help me at all. Then I heard your program on the radio. You talked about God's Son, Jesus. Can he help me? All my family is looking for a new way of life."

George gave the letter to a Venezuelan home missionary. "Maybe you can visit him," he said.

The home missionary took the letter. He looked and looked for the man in the jungle. Just as the sun was setting he stopped his jeep in front of the man's house.

"I am a Baptist missionary," he said. "I represent the radio program, 'Christ, the Only Hope.'"

"I have been waiting for you," the man said. "I want to know who this Jesus is."

42

The home missionary told the man about Jesus.

"This is what I've been looking for," the man said. Right then and there, he accepted Jesus as his Savior.

"What must I do with my books about the spirits?" he asked.

"I can't tell you what to do with them," the home missionary said. "But I think God will let you know what you should do."

The man thought a minute. Then he picked up the books. He carried them to the yard and piled them on the ground. He struck a match and set them on fire. As the last flame died away, the man said, "Now I know who Jesus is. He is my Savior. I feel good inside."

The home missionary told George what had happened. George was glad he had produced the radio program. "Thank you, God," he said in his prayer that day. "Thank you for our radio program and for the people who listen to it."

In 1969 little Lolly was born. Soon afterward, George and Veda Rae took the children to a missionary camp near the seaside. On Sunday morning they went to church on the beach. While one of the missionaries was preaching, three national guardsmen in a jeep stopped nearby.

"I wonder why they stopped," Veda Rae whispered to George. "We've done this every year for many years, and no one has objected. I wonder what can be wrong."

"Paul, go talk to the guardsmen," George said to his son. "Find out what they want."

Paul and the guardsmen talked and talked. After a while, Paul came back. "The men want to know about 'that book' the preacher is using," he said.

Again Veda Rae whispered to George, and George relayed the message to another missionary.

"I have a Spanish New Testament. It's old, but it's still

good. We can give it to them," the missionary said.

Paul took it to the men.

"Tell them to wait," one of the women said. She worked in the Baptist book store. "I have some new New Testaments that we can give to the men."

While she went to get the New Testaments, George talked with the men. One of the guardsmen told him, "Once I was in a meeting where someone was teaching from that book. I liked what I heard. All of us want to know what it says."

George told the men about the Bible and what it says about God.

"A lot of us work here," the guardsman said. "Can someone come and teach us? If they can, we'll have a meeting. We'd meet every week if we had a teacher."

"Someone will be glad to come," George said.

The lady from the book store gave each of the guardsmen a Spanish New Testament. "Thank you," they said. "We'll look forward to hearing more about the things in this book."

As the guardsmen drove away, George and the other missionaries bowed their heads. "Thank you, God, because so many people in Venezuela want to know about you and your book. Thank you for letting us share it with them."

One evening George went home, waving an envelope. It was a letter from the Foreign Mission Board. It said that Baptists in the United States had given enough money to the Lottie Moon Christmas Offering for George to have a new radio studio.

"Now we won't need the egg-carton walls," George told Veda Rae. "We can have a real radio studio."

The Big Voice

George and Veda Rae and their missionary friends looked and looked for a house that would be just right. At last they found it. The upstairs rooms were exactly what George wanted for his radio studio. He began to work on them right away. First of all, he made the walls soundproof. Then he painted them. Soon he moved the recorder, the microphones, and other controls to the new studio.

Very early every morning George went to the studio. And every morning, before he started to work, he read some Bible verses and prayed. One morning he read 2 Corinthians 4:1: "Seeing we have this ministry, as we have received mercy, we faint not."

George thought about what he had read. "God gave us this radio ministry," he said. "And he gives us strength to do it. Sometimes we get tired, but we don't have to give up. God will help us do his work."

George asked a friend to print the verse on a plaque. He hung it in the new studio. He read it every day. It reminded him to keep on working even when it was hard to do so.

One day Veda Rae went to the shopping center. "I want a nice birthday gift for my daughter," she said to the saleslady in the jewelry store. "She is going to be fourteen years old."

"When is her birthday?" the lady asked. "Maybe she

would like a horoscope charm. All the teenagers are wearing them."

"Oh, no," Veda Rae said. "That would never do. We do not believe in horoscopes."

"What do you believe?" the lady asked.

"We believe in Jesus," Veda Rae said. "We believe God loves us and cares for us."

"That sounds like what I hear on the radio," the lady said.

"'Christ, the Only Hope?'" Veda Rae asked.

The lady nodded her head. "Yes, I listen to it every night," she said.

"My husband produces the program," Veda Rae said. "The man who preaches is our friend."

"I always listen to him," the lady said. "I like what he says. Do you know where I can learn more?"

"Where do you live?" Veda Rae asked.

"Los Teques (LOHS TEH-keys)."

"Then you must go to the Baptist Church in Los Teques," Veda Rae said. "I will tell the pastor about you. He will be glad for you to go to his church."

Veda Rae did not buy a gift that day. But when she got home she sent a message to the pastor in Los Teques. She told him about the lady at the jewelry store.

Several days later, Veda Rae went back to the jewelry store.

"I am glad to see you," the lady said. "Now I am a Christian. I am going to be baptized soon. Already I am telling my husband and my son about Jesus."

Veda Rae hugged the lady. "Now we are sisters in Christ," she said. "And God is our Father."

The lady showed Veda Rae a new tray of gifts. "Maybe one of these will please your daughter," she said.

Veda Rae chose some tiny gold earrings. When she got

home, she wrapped them in bright gift paper. On Ann's birthday, she put them at her place on the breakfast table.

"Oh, Mother," Ann exclaimed as she opened the gift. "The earrings are beautiful! I am going to wear them all the time."

At the studio, George received more and more letters from people who listened to the radio program. One was from Esteban Rodríguez (Ehs-TEH-bahn Roh-DREE-guess).

"I have heard your program, 'Christ, the Only Hope,'" he wrote. "I have told my friends about Jesus. Can someone come and help us start a church?"

George and some friends decided to go. They began the trip to Esteban's village. They traveled so far that it seemed they were going to run off the map. At last they reached his house.

Esteban was not at home, so the missionaries visited his family. Soon the neighbors began to arrive. "These people know Jesus, too," Esteban's family said. "Esteban has told them about Jesus."

The missionaries gave Bibles to the people and promised to return.

Four months later the missionaries went back to Esteban's village. The people were still reading the Bible and telling others about Jesus. Almost thirty persons had accepted Jesus as their Savior. While the missionaries were there, they preached, and other people trusted in Jesus.

Esteban was at home when the missionaries went again to the village.

"How did you become a Christian?" the missionaries asked Esteban.

"When I was twenty-two years old," Esteban said, "I went to work in another town. I attended a Christian church and, one day, I trusted in Jesus. Then my job ended. I came back home. When I saw how my family and friends lived, I was ashamed. No one knew I was a Christian. 'Maybe I should go back to my old way of living,' I thought.

"Then I turned on the radio. I heard the 'Christ, the Only Hope' program. It said I should not yield to temptation. Then I knew I should not move away from my village. Instead, I should tell my family and friends about Jesus. They need to accept him as their Savior."

On their way home, the missionaries prayed for Esteban. They thanked God for the radio and for the "Christ, the Only Hope" broadcast.

George looked at the plaque on the studio wall. "Now, I feel encouraged again," he said. Then he looked at his desk. It was covered with letters. Two hundred and fifty of them! "How can I ever answer all of them?" he said.

That night George told Veda Rae about all the letters they were getting. "They must be answered," he said. "But there is no money for a secretary." Then he thought a minute. "Do you suppose you could be the secretary?" he asked.

"I can try," she said.

One by one, Veda Rae answered the letters. Sometimes she sent a Bible, a New Testament, or a Bible study lesson with the letters. Every time she read a letter from someone who had heard about Jesus on the radio, she thanked God.

One of the letters she answered was from Mrs. Aray (Ah-RAH-ee). "One night I was very tired," Mrs. Aray wrote. "My husband is paralyzed. I raise animals and sell them to make a living for my family. That night I turned the radio on. I heard quiet music. Then the speaker explained how I could make contact with God just by trusting Jesus.

"I knelt down and asked Christ to be my Savior and

Lord. Now I read the Bible every day. Jesus fills my home with rich blessings."

Veda Rae sent Mrs. Aray a copy of the Bible study course. Mrs. Aray studied it. Every time Mrs. Aray finished a lesson, she mailed it to Veda Rae. Veda Rae corrected the lessons and returned them to her.

One day Mrs. Aray visited the Central Baptist Church in Caracas. "I believe in Jesus," she told the pastor. "Can you baptize me?"

The pastor talked to Mrs. Aray. He asked her questions to see what she understood about being a Christian.

"Everything I know is what I have learned from the Bible," she said. "We do not have a Baptist church in our village."

After the pastor baptized her, she went home and told her husband about Jesus. He, too, became a Christian. She told her neighbors about Jesus. Some of them also believed.

Later, some preachers visited the Aray family. They preached several times, and thirty people became Christians.

One of the preachers saw a woman hanging clothes on a line in her backyard. He told her about Jesus. She accepted Jesus as her Savior. Then she turned to a neighbor who was listening over the fence.

"Why don't you accept Jesus, too?" she said. "I know you have many problems. Only Jesus can help you."

Many people came to the Aray's house to study the Bible. When there were too many to get inside, Mrs. Aray cleaned her chicken house and used it for a preaching room. Soon more than sixty people in her village believed in Jesus.

"Please, send us a preacher," she begged. A seminary student heard about the Aray family. He agreed to visit them every weekend. The group grew and grew. Soon it became a Baptist mission.

Veda Rae continued to hear from Mrs. Aray and was encouraged. "It's wonderful," she thought. God is using the big voice of radio to tell many people about his love. I'm glad he lets me help by answering the letters."

During the first ten months she worked as secretary, Veda Rae answered 2,500 letters. Soon she was receiving 400 letters every month. Many came from Cuba, Ecuador, and other countries. Just before Christmas, George offered a calendar with colored Bible pictures to all who wrote for one. Then, Veda Rae received 400 letters a week.

In one year 150 people who listened to the radio program accepted Jesus as their Savior.

Flash Flood

The day began as every school day began in Caracas. Veda Rae got Larry and Lolly off to school. Then, she and George waved to Ann as they left the house for the radio studio. Ann was home from college. Veda Rae knew she would take care of the house and be there when Larry and Lolly got home in the afternoon.

The skies were cloudy, but that, too, was not unusual. Sometimes it seemed to rain every day.

George drove carefully through the heavy traffic. At the office he began to record a new radio program. Veda Rae tackled a stack of letters and Bible study lessons.

It rained off and on all day. Visitors stopped by and talked about the rain. "We heard on the radio that the river has flooded in several parts of town. How is it where you live?" they said.

"I'm sure everything is all right," Veda Rae said. "Ann is at home. She would call if anything has happened."

At quitting time, the rain stopped. Already the clouds were lifting. Veda Rae and George could almost see the top of the mountains.

But the nearer home they got, the more water they found in the streets. Then they saw the mud. Even the bridge near their house was covered with a foot of the dirty slush.

52

Bulldozers were trying to scrape it off, but many cars were stalled along the way.

George inched the car across the bridge and down the street. As he turned into their driveway, the lights of the car flashed against the wall of the house.

"George, look! There are streaks of mud on the wall all the way to the top of the windows!" Veda Rae said. "The flood we heard about must have come through here."

George parked the car in the garage. Carefully, he and Veda Rae waded through the muddy yard to the front door. The house was dark.

"I wonder where the children are," Veda Rae said.

"Probably at a friend's house," George said, but he wasn't at all sure.

Then he flicked on the light and saw the mess. Mud, thick, sticky, smelly mud, everywhere. Tables and chairs were piled upside down in the middle of the floor and were covered with mud. Even the piano was on its side and half hidden in the sticky gook. Muddy water still dripped from the pictures on the walls.

George grabbed the phone. It, too, was wet and muddy. "I'll call our missionary friends. The children know to go there if they need something. Maybe they are there," he said. He dialed the number, but the phone was dead.

Just then the front door opened cautiously. "Who's here?" a voice called from the outside.

"Ann? Lolly? Is that you?" Veda Rae called. She rushed to the door. "What happened?" she asked as she hugged the girls.

"Oh, Mom," Lolly cried. "The water started coming in under the kitchen door, and we couldn't stop it." She still cuddled her wet puppy in her arms.

"The water came in, faster and faster," Ann said. "I tried

to call you, but the phone was dead. All I could get was a loud, crackling noise. By that time, the water was nearly to the top of the stairs."

"How did you get out?" George wanted to know.

"I thought about the balcony," Ann said, "but I forgot there were new security bars on the windows."

"We were standing on the stairs watching the water as it filled the room below. Then we saw the *pilón*, the one like the country people use to grind corn. It came floating along on top of the water near the stairs," Ann continued.

"The *pilón*?" Veda Rae exclaimed. "It must weigh a hundred pounds!"

"I know," Ann replied. "But I remembered Dad had said people use the same kind of wood to make canoes. So, I tried pushing it down. It bobbed up again. It still floated."

"She made me and my puppy get on first," Lolly said. "Then she got on behind us. We rode the *pilón* like a horse and paddled with our feet out an upstairs window."

"We had to duck our heads to get through the door, but we made it," Ann said. "Outside, we climbed to the top of the wall and from there to the roof."

"The neighbors were on their roofs, too," Lolly said. "We talked to them. Then the water went down real fast, and we came down."

"The firemen came by," Ann said. "But when they saw we were all right, they went on to help someone else. I took Lolly and the puppy and went across the bridge to the other missionaries' house. They weren't at home, so we came on back. And you were here." Ann sighed.

"And Larry? Where's he?" George asked.

"I don't know," Ann answered wearily. "He didn't come on the early bus. I hope he stopped at a friend's house. I just hope he didn't get caught in the flood."

"George! Veda Rae!" New voices called from the front gate.

What a welcome sound! Other missionaries and friends from the church in another part of town were there. And right in the middle of the group was Larry!

"Mom! Dad!" He hugged them tightly. "I was so afraid all of you had drowned. I got home on the late bus and found all this mess. Nobody was here, so I left a note and went to a friend's house."

The note was where Larry had left it, but in the confusion, no one had found it.

"Well!" one of the friends said. "Heave to! Everybody's safe. Now, let's get this mud out of here."

All night long they worked. And all the next day. When everything was clean and the friends had gone home, George looked at Veda Rae. "Aren't friends nice?" he said.

"Yes," Veda Rae said. "And isn't God good? Just think, he took care of our children in the flood. He helped them know what to do."

Good-byes Are Not Forever

It was almost furlough time again. Only, this time it was different. George and Veda Rae would not be going back to Venezuela.

"We want you to go to Ecuador," the Foreign Mission Board had said. "The missionaries there need you."

"If that is what God wants us to do, we will," George said. "A young Venezuelan man is ready to do the radio work. Veda Rae's helper knows how to answer the letters. We are ready to go wherever God needs us."

It was not easy to say good-bye. But Veda Rae began to pack. This time everything—clothes, TV, piano, furniture—had to go.

Neighbors stopped by. "We do not want you to leave," they said. "You are our friends. You have told us about Jesus. We will miss you."

Even at church, the people were sad. "You have been our helper. How can we let you go?" they said. The church gave a banquet for them. George talked to the people. "Do you remember the plaque on the studio wall?" he said. "It says, 'Seeing we have this ministry, as we have received mercy, we faint not' (2 Corinthians 4:1). The work at the studio and in the churches is your work, too. God has given it to you. He will help you do it. You must not lose heart."

Veda Rae knew George was right. Still, saying good-bye was not easy. Then she remembered the Bible verse she had read in Manor, Texas. "Be strong and of a good courage. . . . The Lord, he it is that doth go before thee; he will be with thee, he will not fail thee, neither forsake thee: fear not, neither be dismayed" (Deuteronomy 31:7-8).

On June 18, 1982 George, Veda Rae, Larry, and Lolly waved good-bye to Venezuela. Only Ann stayed to finish her job. Then she, too, returned to Texas.

For six months between assignments, George and Veda Rae visited their family and friends. Paul and Mark were grown. Paul worked in real estate on Padre Island. Mark was a teller in a bank in Austin, Texas. Larry would stay in the United States to study at Baylor. Only Lolly would go to Ecuador with George and Veda Rae.

Just three weeks before time to say good-bye again, George and Veda Rae's first grandchild was born. Mark and his wife Carolyn had a baby girl and named her Kimberly Ann. Veda Rae cuddled her in her arms. "It's great to be a grandmother," she said.

The Lozuks had been in Quito (KEY-toh), Ecuador, only a few days when two missionary women invited Veda Rae to make a visit with them.

Inside a tiny room, Veda Rae met a young Indian woman. Her name was Laura, and she had been sick for nine months. Her mother tried to take care of her and her four little children. The missionaries gave her some medicine. They also talked to her about Jesus.

The next week the missionaries visited Laura again. This time Laura was in bed. She tried to sit up to greet the missionaries, but she was very weak.

"Would you like for us to sing a song about Jesus?" the missionaries said.

"Sí (SEE, Yes)," Laura whispered. "Please sing 'Quédate aquí, Señor' (KEH-dah-teh ah-KEY, Seh-NIOR, Stay here, Lord)."

Sometimes the missionaries forgot the Spanish words,

but Laura sang them, every one.

At home, Veda Rae talked with George about Laura. A few days later, Laura died. "I'm glad we could tell her about Jesus," Veda Rae said.

"Yes," George said. "Maybe you'd like to hear about the Indian man in Paute (Pah-OO-teh). Today, one of the missionaries told me about him. When the man took his shoes to be mended, he saw a poster about a Baptist church on the cobbler's wall.

"The man asked where the church met. 'Here in my house,' the cobbler said. Then, the man told the cobbler that he had been reading the Bible for ten years. He asked if someone could go to his town and teach him and his family about God."

"Maybe, sometime, we can go," Veda Rae suggested.

Veda Rae and George looked out the window. From their apartment they saw the rooftops of houses below. They looked across the city. In the distance they saw the mountains. Some of them were so high they were covered with snow.

"Just think," Veda Rae said. "Everything seems different. In Venezuela we lived in a house near a river that flooded. Here in Ecuador we live in an apartment on the eighth floor. In Venezuela we lived near the ocean. Here we live in the mountains. But some things are just the same. The people here speak Spanish just like the people in Venezuela. And they need to know Jesus just the same."

Then they knew it was true. Good-byes are not forever. They are just the beginning of another wonderful, new part of living.

Veda Rae and George bowed their heads. "Thank you, God, for bringing us here. We are glad you want us to share your love with these new friends in Ecuador."

60

Important Dates in the Lives of George and Veda Rae Lozuk

George's birth: November 25, 1928

Veda Rae's birth: December 14, 1928

George's acceptance of Jesus as Savior: 1938

Veda Rae's acceptance of Jesus as Savior: 1936

George's ordination: January 1949

George and Veda Rae were married: June 2, 1950

George and Veda Rae were summer missionaries in California: June-September 1950

George and Veda Rae were appointed by the Foreign Mission Board: May 10, 1956

George and Veda Rae went to Spanish language school in Costa Rica: 1956-1957

George and Veda Rae arrived in Venezuela: October 17, 1957

George became radio technician and programmer for Baptists in Venezuela: 1967

Veda Rae began radio follow-up work in Venezuela: 1970

George and Veda Rae were transferred to Ecuador: September 1, 1982

Remember?

In the Bible God tells us to be "doers of the word, and not hearers only" (James 1:22). What do you think this means? Could it mean that we are to obey God instead of just reading or listening to what he says?

Here is a list of things that can help us know what God wants us to do. Which ones helped George and Veda Rae? Which ones can help you?

- Read the Bible.
- Go to Sunday School.
- Listen to the pastor's sermons.
- Ask God to show you what he wants you to do.
- Talk about it with your parents, teachers at church, and your pastor.

How did George and Veda Rae obey God:

- When they were children? (See chapters 1 and 2.)
- When they were in college? (See chapter 3.)
- When they were in Venezuela? (See chapters 6, 7, and 8.)
- When they were in Ecuador? (See chapter 10.)

How did they know God wanted them to accept Jesus as their Savior? (See chapters 1 and 2.)

How did they know God wanted them to be missionaries? (See chapters 3 and 5.)

How can you obey God? Maybe you want to accept Jesus

as your Savior. Or perhaps you think God is calling you to be a missionary, a pastor, or another special worker for him. If so, pray to God. Tell him what you are thinking. Ask him to help you know what he wants you to do. Then talk with your parents, your teachers at church, and your pastor. They can help you understand what you are feeling. Then you can decide how you can obey God and do what he wants you to do.

About the Author

Roberta Ryan is a foreign missionary who lives and works in the United States. She is a book editor at the Baptist Spanish Publishing House, El Paso, Texas. Sometimes she teaches boys and girls in the Spanish missions in El Paso.

Before Miss Ryan moved to El Paso, she was a missionary in South America. She taught in the mission school in Temuco, Chile. She also wrote and edited missionary magazines in Spanish for boys and girls.

Miss Ryan has written other books for children: *Who? Me? Keep Telling the Story, The Claim Staker,* and, in Spanish, *Las Aventuras de Pelú (The Adventures of Pelú).*

Date Due

Code 4386-04, CLS-4, Broadman Supplies, Nashville, Tenn.,
Printed in U.S.A.